SAMUEL COLERIDGE-TAYLOR

Hiawatha's Wedding Feast

No 1 from OPUS 30: 'SONG OF HIAWATHA'

Cantata for tenor solo, SATB & orchestra

Words by H. W. Longfellow

Dedicated 'To Sir George Grove, C.B.
as a slight token of sincerest affection,
respect and admiration.'

Order No: NOV 07 2301

NOVELLO PUBLISHING LIMITED

SCENES FROM THE SONG OF HIAWATHA.

I. HIAWATHA'S WEDDING FEAST.

You shall hear how Pau-Puk-Keewis,
How the handsome Yenadizze,
Danced at Hiawatha's wedding ;
How the gentle Chibiabos,
He the sweetest of musicians,
Sang his songs of love and longing ;
How Iagoo, the great boaster,
He the marvellous storyteller,
Told his tales of strange adventure,
That the feast might be more joyous,
That the time might pass more gaily,
And the guests be more contented.
    Sumptuous was the feast Nokomis
Made at Hiawatha's wedding.
All the bowls were made of bass-wood,
White and polished very smoothly,
All the spoons of horn of bison,
Black and polished very smoothly.
    She had sent through all the village
Messengers with wands of willow,
As a sign of invitation,
As a token of the feasting ;
And the wedding-guests assembled,
Clad in all their richest raiment,
Robes of fur and belts of wampum,
Splendid with their paint and plumage,
Beautiful with beads and tassels.
    First they ate the sturgeon, Nahma,
And the pike, the Maskenozha,
Caught and cooked by old Nokomis,
Then on pemican they feasted,
Pemican and buffalo marrow,
Haunch of deer and hump of bison,
Yellow cakes of the Mondamin,
And the wild rice of the river.
    But the gracious Hiawatha,
And the lovely Laughing Water,
And the careful old Nokomis,
Tasted not the food before them,
Only waited on the others,
Only served their guests in silence.
    And when all the guests had finished,
Old Nokomis, brisk and busy,

From an ample pouch of otter,
Filled the red stone pipes for smoking
With tobacco from the South-land,
Mixed with bark of the red willow,
And with herbs and leaves of fragrance.
    Then she said, "O Pau-Puk-Keewis,
Dance for us your merry dances,
Dance the Beggar's Dance to please us,
That the feast may be more joyous,
That the time may pass more gaily,
And our guests be more contented !"
    Then the handsome Pau-Puk-Keewis,
He the idle Yenadizze,
He the merry mischief-maker,
Whom the people called the Storm-Fool,
Rose among the guests assembled.
    Skilled was he in sports and pastimes,
In the merry dance of snow-shoes,
In the play of quoits and ball-play ;
Skilled was he in games of hazard,
In all games of skill and hazard,
Pugasaing, the Bowl and Counters,
Koomtassoo, the Game of Plum-stones.
    Though the warriors called him Faint-Heart,
Called him coward, Shaugodaya,
Idler, gambler, Yenadizze,
Little heeded he their jesting,
Little cared he for their insults,
For the women and the maidens
Loved the handsome Pau-Puk-Keewis.
    He was dressed in shirt of doe-skin,
White and soft, and fringed with ermine,
All inwrought with beads of wampum ;
He was dressed in deer-skin leggings,
Fringed with hedgehog quills and ermine,
And in mocassins of buck-skin
Thick with quills and beads embroidered.
On his head were plumes of swan's down,
On his heels were tails of foxes,
In one hand a fan of feathers,
And a pipe was in the other.
    Barred with streaks of red and yellow,
Streaks of blue and bright vermilion,

Shone the face of Pau-Puk-Keewis.
From his forehead fell his tresses.
Smooth and parted like a woman's.
Shining bright with oil, and plaited,
Hung with braids of scented grasses,
As among the guests assembled,
To the sound of flutes and singing,
To the sounds of drums and voices,
Rose the handsome Pau-Puk-Keewis,
And began his mystic dances.

First he danced a solemn measure,
Very slow in step and gesture,
In and out among the pine trees,
Through the shadows and the sunshine,
Treading softly like a panther,
Then more swiftly and still swifter,
Whirling, spinning round in circles,
Leaping o'er the guests assembled,
Eddying round and round the wigwam,
Till the leaves went whirling with him,
Till the dust and wind together
Swept in eddies round about him.

Then along the sandy margin
Of the lake, the Big-Sea-Water,
On he sped with frenzied gestures,
Stamped upon the sand, and tossed it
Wildly in the air around him;
Till the wind became a whirlwind,
Till the sand was blown and sifted
Like great snowdrifts o'er the landscape,
Heaping all the shores with Sand Dunes,
Sand Hills of the Nagow Wudjoo!

Thus the merry Pau-Puk-Keewis
Danced his Beggar's Dance to please them,
And, returning, sat down laughing
There among the guests assembled.
Sat and fanned himself serenely
With his fan of turkey-feathers.

Then they said to Chibiabos,
To the friend of Hiawatha,
To the sweetest of all singers.
To the best of all musicians,
" Sing to us, O Chibiabos!
Songs of love and songs of longing,
That the feast may be more joyous,
That the time may pass more gaily,
And our guests be more contented! "

And the gentle Chibiabos
Sang in accents sweet and tender,
Sang in tones of deep emotion,
Songs of love and songs of longing,
Looking still at Hiawatha,
Looking at fair Laughing Water,
Sang he softly, sang in this wise:

" Onaway! Awake, beloved!
Thou the wild-flower of the forest!
Thou the wild-bird of the prairie!
Thou with eyes so soft and fawn-like!
" If thou only lookest at me,

I am happy, I am happy,
As the lilies of the prairie,
When they feel the dew upon them!
" Sweet thy breath is as the fragrance
Of the wild-flowers in the morning,
As their fragrance is at evening,
In the Moon when leaves are falling.
" Does not all the blood within me
Leap to meet thee, leap to meet thee,
As the springs to meet the sunshine,
In the Moon when nights are brightest?
" Onaway! my heart sings to thee,
Sings with joy when thou art near me,
As the sighing, singing branches
In the pleasant Moon of Strawberries!
" When thou art not pleased, beloved,
Then my heart is sad and darkened,
As the shining river darkens
When the clouds drop shadows on it!
" When thou smilest, my beloved,
Then my troubled heart is brightened,
As in sunshine gleam the ripples
That the cold wind makes in rivers.
" Smiles the earth, and smile the waters
Smile the cloudless skies above us,
But I lose the way of smiling
When thou art no longer near me!
" I myself, myself! behold me!
Blood of my beating heart, behold me!
O awake, awake, beloved!
Onaway! awake, beloved! "

Thus the gentle Chibiabos
Sang his song of love and longing;
And Iagoo, the great boaster,
He the marvellous storyteller,
He the friend of old Nokomis,
Jealous of the sweet musician,
Jealous of the applause they gave him,
Saw in all the eyes around him,
Saw in all their looks and gestures,
That the wedding-guests assembled
Longed to hear his pleasant stories,
His immeasurable falsehoods.

Very boastful was Iagoo:
Never heard he an adventure
But himself had made a greater;
Never any deed of daring
But himself had done a bolder;
Never any marvellous story
But himself could tell a stranger.

Would you listen to his boasting,
Would you only give him credence,
No one ever shot an arrow
Half so far and high as he had;
Ever caught so many fishes,
Ever killed so many reindeer,
Ever trapped so many beaver!

None could run so fast as he could,
None could dive so deep as he could,

None could swim so far as he could;
None had made so many journeys,
None had seen so many wonders,
As this wonderful Iagoo,
As this marvellous storyteller!
    Thus his name became a by-word
And a jest among the people!
And whene'er a boastful hunter
Praised his own address too highly,
Or a warrior, home returning,
Talked too much of his achievements,
All his hearers cried, " Iagoo!
Here's Iagoo come among us!"
    He it was who carved the cradle
Of the little Hiawatha,
Carved its framework out of linden,
Bound it strong with reindeer's sinews:
He it was who taught him later
How to make his bows and arrows,
How to make the bows of ash-tree,
And the arrows of the oak-tree.
So among the guests assembled

At my Hiawatha's wedding
Sat Iagoo, old and ugly,
Sat the marvellous storyteller.
    And they said, " O good Iagoo,
Tell us now a tale of wonder,
Tell us of some strange adventure,
That the feast may be more joyous,
That the time may pass more gaily,
And our guests be more contented!"
    And Iagoo answered straightway,
" You shall hear a tale of wonder,
You shall hear of strange adventures."
So he told the strange adventures
Of Osseo, the Magician,
From the Evening Star descended.

    Such was Hiawatha's Wedding,
Thus the wedding-banquet ended,
And the wedding-guests departed,
Leaving Hiawatha happy
With the night and Minnehaha.

Hiawa'tha, *the Prophet, the Teacher; son of Mudjekeewis, the West-Wind, and Wenonah, daughter of Nokomis.*

Minneha'ha, *Laughing Water; wife of Hiawatha.*

Pau-Puk-Kee'wis, *the handsome Yenadizze, the Storm-Fool.*

Yenadiz'ze, *an idler and gambler; an Indian dandy.*

Chibia'bos, *a musician; friend of Hiawatha, Ruler in the Land of Spirits.*

Ia'goo, *a great boaster and storyteller.*

Noko'mis, *grandmother of Hiawatha; mother of Wenonah.*

Nah'ma, *the sturgeon.*

Maskeno'zha, *the pike.*

Pem'ican, *meat of the deer or buffalo, dried and pounded.*

Monda'min, *Indian corn.*

Pugasaing', *the game of bowl and counters.*

Koomtassoo', *the game of plum-stones.*

Shaugada'ya, *a coward.*

Na'gow Wudjoo', *the Sand Dunes of Lake Superior.*

Onaway', *awake.*

Osse'o, *Son of the Evening Star.*

SCENES FROM THE SONG OF HIAWATHA.

I. HIAWATHA'S WEDDING FEAST.

LONGFELLOW.

S. COLERIDGE-TAYLOR (Op. 30, No. 1).

You shall hear how Pau-Puk-Kee-wis, How the handsome Ye - na-diz-ze, Danced at Hi-a-wa-tha's

You shall hear how Pau-Puk-Kee-wis, How the handsome Ye - na-diz-ze, Danced at Hi-a-wa-tha's

wed-ding;

wed-ding;

How the gen-tle Chi-bi-a-bos,

How the gen-tle Chi-bi-a-bos,

He the sweet-est of mu-sic-ians, Sang his songs of love and longing;

He the sweet-est of mu-sic-ians, Sang his songs of love and longing;

8285.

joy-ous, That the time . . might pass more gai-ly, And the guests be more con-

joy-ous, That the time might pass more gai-ly, And the guests be more con-

joy-ous, That the time might pass more gai-ly, And the guests be more con-

joy-ous, That the time might pass more gai-ly, And the guests . . be more con-

- tent-ed. Sumptuous was the feast No - ko-mis Made at Hi - a -

- tent - ed. Sumptuous was the feast No - ko-mis Made at Hi - a -

- tent - ed. Sumptuous was the feast No - ko-mis Made at Hi - a -

- tent - ed. Sumptuous was the feast No - ko-mis Made at Hi - a -

- wa - tha's wedding.

- wa - tha's wedding.

- wa - tha's wedding.

- wa - tha's wedding.

All the bowls were made of bass-wood, White and

All the bowls were made of bass-wood, White and

All the spoons of horn of bis-on, Black and polished ve-ry

All the spoons of horn of bis-on, Black and polished ve-ry

polished ve-ry smoothly,

polished ve-ry smoothly,

smoothly. She had sent . . . Mes-sengers with wands of wil-low,

smoothly. Mes-sengers with wands of wil-low,

She had sent thro' all the vil-lage Mes-sengers with wands of wil-low,

She had sent thro' all the vil-lage Messengers with wands of wil-low,

As a sign, ... As a

As a sign of in-vi-ta-tion, As a

As a sign of in-vi-ta-tion, As a

Str. & Wood.

L.H.

f cres. molto.

ff

to-ken;   And the wed-ding - guests as-semb-led,

to-ken of the feast-ing;   And the guests . . . . .

to-ken of the feast-ing;   And the guests . . . . .

f Wood-Wind only.

Clad in all their rich-est rai-ments,

Clad in all their rich-est rai-ments,

. . . as - semb - led,

add Str. ———— sf

8285.

8

First they ate the stur-geon, Nah-ma, And the pike, the

First they ate the stur-geon, And the

First they ate the stur-geon, And the

First they ate the stur-geon, And the

Str.

Mas - ken - oz - ha, Caught and cooked by old No-ko-mis,

Mas - ken - oz - ha, Caught, cooked, by old No-ko-mis,

Mas - ken - oz - ha, Caught, cooked, by old No-ko-mis,

Mas - ken - oz - ha, Caught, cooked, by old No-ko-mis,

On pem - i - can they feast - ed,

On pem - i - can they feast - ed,

Then on pem - i - can . . . they feast - ed,

Then on pem - i - can . . . they feast - ed,

And buf - fa - lo mar - row, Haunch of deer and

And buf - fa - lo mar - row, Haunch of deer and

Pem - i - can and buf - fa - lo . . . mar - row, Haunch of deer and

Pem - i - can and buf - fa - lo . . . mar - row, Haunch of deer and

hump of bis - on, Yel - low cakes of the Mon - da - min,

hump of bis - on, Yel - low cakes of the Mon - da - min,

hump of bis - on, Yel - low cakes of the Mon - da - min,

hump of bis - on, Yel - low cakes of the Mon - da - min,

8285.

8285.

13

Call'd him coward, Shau - go-da-ya,

I - dler, gambler, Ye - na-diz-ze,

call'd him Faint-heart,

Lit - tle heed-ed he their jest - ing,

For the wo - men and the maid - ens

For the wo - men and the maid - ens

Lit-tle car'd he for their in - sults, For the wo - men and the maid - ens

For the wo - men and the maid - ens

8285.

He was dress'd in shirt of doe-skin, White and soft, and fring'd with er-mine,

All in-wrought with beads of wam-pum;

On his heels were tails of fox-es, In one hand a fan of fea-thers,

On his heels were tails of fox-es, In one hand a fan of fea-thers,

28

And a pipe was in the o-ther.

And a pipe was in the o-ther.

TENORS.

And a pipe was in the o-ther.

BASSES.

And a pipe was in the o-ther.

28

8285.

24

29

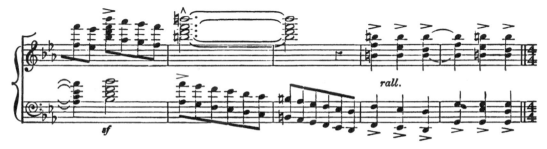

38 *Molto pesante.*
sempre ff

Thus the mer - ry Pau-Puk - Kee-wis Danc'd his Beg-gar's Dance to please them,

sempre ff

Thus the mer - ry Pau-Puk - Kee-wis Danc'd his Beg-gar's Dance to please them,

sempre ff

Thus the mer - ry Pau-Puk - Kee-wis Danc'd his Beg-gar's Dance to please them,

sempre ff

Thus the mer - ry Pau-Puk - Kee-wis Danc'd his Beg-gar's Dance to please them,

38 *Molto pesante.* $\quad \bullet = 130.$

sempre ff *Tutti.*

32

Then said they to Chi-bi-a-bos, To the friend of Hi-a-

Then said they to Chi-bi-a-bos, To the friend of Hi-a-

Then said they to Chi-bi-a-bos, To the friend ot Hi-a-

Then said they to Chi-bi-a-bos, To the friend of Hi-a-

- a - bos! Songs of love and songs of long - ing, That the feast may be more

- a - bos! Songs of love and songs of long - ing, That the feast may be more

- a - bos! Songs of love and songs of long - ing, That . . . the feast may be more

- a - bos! Songs of love and songs of long - ing, That the feast may be more

joy - ous, That the time may pass more gai - ly, And our guests be

joy - ous, That the time may pass more gai - ly, And our guests be

joy - ous, That the time may pass more gai - ly, And our guests be

joy - ous, That the time may pass more gai - ly, And our guests be

more con - tent - ed!"

more con - tent - ed!" .. And the gen - tle

more con - tent - ed!" .. The

more con - tent - ed!" ..

Str. con sord.

Hi - a - wa - tha, Look - ing at fair . . Laugh - ing Wa - ter,

sostenuto.
pp
With Trombones.

rall. . . poco . . a . . poco.
pp
Sang he soft - ly, . . Sang in this wise: . .

rall.
pp
Sang he soft - ly, . . Sang in this wise: . .

rall.
pp
Sang he soft - ly, . . Sang in this wise: . .

rall.
pp
Sang he soft - ly, . . Sang in this wise: . .

rall. . poco . a . . poco.

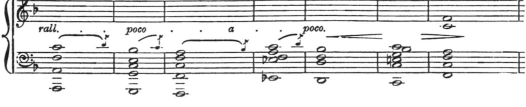

Fl.

mor - - en - - do.

Str. & Cor.

8285. Ped.

sun - shine gleam the rip - ples That the cold wind makes in riv - ers...

Smiles the earth, and smile the wa - ters, Smile the cloudless skies a-bove us, But

I . . lose the way of smi - ling When thou art no long-er near me! . . .

a tempo.

I my -

8285.

42

8285.

8285.

So a-mong the guests as-semb-led At my Hi - a - wa - tha's wedding Sat I -

So a-mong the guests as-semb-led At my Hi - a - wa - tha's wedding Sat I -

So a-mong the guests as-semb-led At my Hi - a - wa - tha's wedding Sat I -

So a-mong the guests as-semb-led At my Hi - a - wa - tha's wedding Sat I -

Str. Wood & Cor.

- a-goo, old and ug-ly, Sat the marv'llous sto-ry - tel-ler.

- a-goo, old and ug-ly, Sat the marv'llous sto-ry - tel-ler.

- a-goo, old and ug-ly, Sat the marv'llous sto-ry - tel-ler.

- a-goo, old and ug-ly, Sat the marv'llous sto-ry - tel-ler.

stretto.

Ped. *Ped.*

Molto più mosso. ♩ = 180.

fff ben marcato.

Ped. *Ped.* *Ped.*

with Brass, Drums, & Cymbals.

8285.

74 mf Meno mosso.
Such was Hi - a - wa - tha's wed-ding, Thus the wed-ding-banquet
Such was Hi - a - wa - tha's wed-ding, Thus the ban - quet
Such was Hi - a - wa - tha's wed-ding, Thus the ban - quet
Such was Hi - a - wa - tha's wed-ding, Thus the ban - quet
74 Meno mosso.
mf sostenuto. Str. Cl. Ob. & Fag.
end - ed, And the wed - ding-guests de - part - ed, Leav - ing
end - ed, And the guests . . . de - part - ed, Leav - ing
end - ed, And the guests . . . de - part - ed, Leav - ing
end - ed, And the wed - ding guests de - part - ed, Leav - ing
mor - - - - - - en - - - - - do. 75
Hi - - - a - wa - tha hap - py, . . . hap - py
Hi - - a - wa - tha hap - py, hap - py
Hi - - a - wa - tha hap - py, hap - py
Hi - - - a - wa - tha hap - py, hap - py
75
mor - - - - - - en - - - - - do.

With the night . . . . and Min-ne - ha - - ha. . . . .

With the night and Min - ne - ha - - ha. . .

With the night and Min - ne - ha - - ha. . .

With the night and Min - ne - ha - - ha. . . .

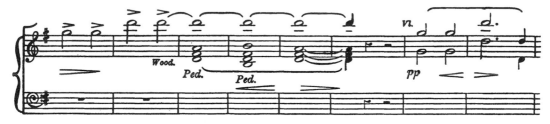